DELTA FORCE

Simon Rose

P9-CBF-443

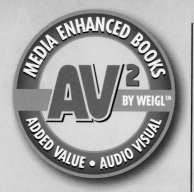

AV² provides enriched content that supplements and complements this book. Weigl's AV² books strive to create inspired learning and engage young minds in a total learning experience.

Your AV² Media Enhanced books come alive with...

Audio
Listen to sections of the book read aloud.

Key Words
Study vocabulary, and complete a matching word activity.

Go to www.av2books.com, and enter this book's unique code.

Video
Watch informative video clips.

Quizzes
Test your knowledge.

BOOK CODE

N 8 4 9 6 9 0

Embedded Weblinks
Gain additional information for research.

Slide Show
View images and captions, and prepare a presentation.

AV² by Weigl brings you media enhanced books that support active learning.

Try This!
Complete activities and hands-on experiments.

... and much, much more!

Published by AV² by Weigl
350 5th Avenue, 59th Floor
New York, NY 10118
Website: www.av2books.com www.weigl.com

Library of Congress Cataloging-in-Publication Data
Rose, Simon, 1961-
Delta Force / Simon Rose.
    p. cm. -- (U.S. Armed Forces)
Audience: Grades 4-6.
Includes index.
ISBN 978-1-62127-450-6 (hbk. : alk. paper) -- ISBN 978-1-62127-456-8 (pbk. : alk. paper)
1. United States. Army. Delta Force--Juvenile literature. 2. United States. Army--Commando troops--Juvenile literature. I. Title.
UA34.S64R67 2014
356'.1670973--dc23
                    2012040423

Printed in the United States of America in North Mankato, Minnesota
1 2 3 4 5 6 7 8 9 0   17 16 15 14 13

022013
WEP301112

Project Coordinator: Aaron Carr
Designer: Mandy Christiansen

Photo Credits
Due to the highly secretive nature of the work carried out by Delta Force, any photos of actual Delta Force operators have been modified to obscure their identities. All other photos used in this book are model-released stock images. They are meant to serve as accurate representations of U.S. Special Operations personnel, even though the people in the photos may not be special operators. Weigl acknowledges Getty Images, iStockphoto, Dreamstime, Alamy, and the U.S. Department of Defense as the primary image suppliers for this book.

Every reasonable effort has been made to trace ownership and to obtain permission to reprint copyright material. The publisher would be pleased to have any errors or omissions brought to their attention so that they may be corrected in subsequent printings.

CONTENTS

WHAT IS DELTA FORCE?

Delta Force is a top-secret special operations division of the United States Army. It is officially known as 1st Special Forces Operational Detachment-Delta (1st SFOD-D). Along with the Navy SEALs **DEVGRU** unit, Delta Force is among the most elite of the U.S. Special Operations.

Delta Force is one of three Army divisions of the United States Special Operations Command (USSOCOM). The others are the Army Rangers and the Green Berets. The Department of Defense is in charge of all the branches of the Armed Forces except the Coast Guard. Information about Delta Force and its missions are mostly secret. There are thought to be between 800 and 1,000 personnel in Delta Force.

★ Though Delta Force is a unit of Army Special Operations Command (ASOC), their missions often fall under the command of the Joint Special Operations Command (JSOC).

USSOCOM Organizational Structure

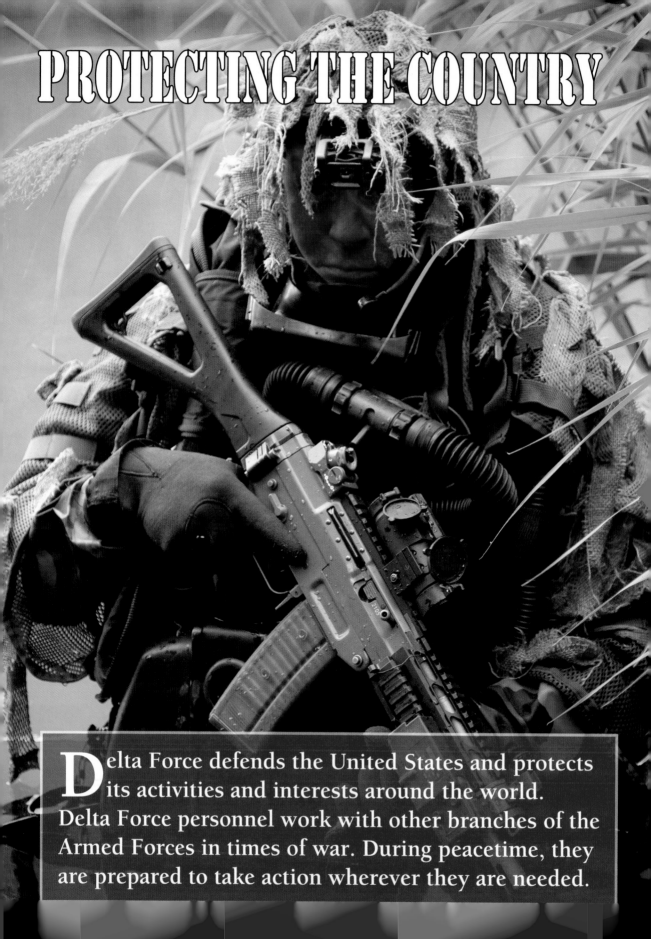

PROTECTING THE COUNTRY

Delta Force defends the United States and protects its activities and interests around the world. Delta Force personnel work with other branches of the Armed Forces in times of war. During peacetime, they are prepared to take action wherever they are needed.

Most details about Delta Force are **classified information** and not available to the public. Delta Force is believed to consist of three or four groups, called squadrons. These are divided into smaller groups called troops. Each troop has specialists with different skills, such as **snipers**, parachutists, and technology experts.

On the Front Lines

On the battlefield, Delta Force operators are involved in operations on the ground. They mostly take part in unconventional warfare, such as secret missions behind enemy lines, **reconnaissance**, capturing enemy leaders, rescuing **hostages**, and fighting **terrorism.** Some Delta Force missions prepare the way for larger attacks by the U.S. Armed Forces.

DELTA FORCE FACTS

The 1st Special Forces Operational Detachment-Delta (1st SFOD-D) is known as Delta Force to most people. Members of Delta Force usually refer to themselves as The Unit. They also refer to themselves as "operators" rather than soldiers.

Delta Force operators are expert sharpshooters. It is believed that they must be able to shoot with 100 percent accuracy from 600 yards (550 meters) away to join the force.

HISTORY OF DELTA FORCE

Most of Delta Force's work is top secret. However, details of some operations have been released to the general public, including in the wars and missions listed here.

1977
★ The 1st Special Forces Operational Detachment-Delta (1st SFOD-D), known as Delta Force, is founded

1983
★ Invasion of Grenada

1980
★ Delta Force operators attempt to rescue American hostages in Tehran, Iran

1989
★ Delta Force takes part in the invasion of Panama

1980

1989

Over the years, Delta Force has planned many more missions than it has actually carried out. In most cases, the reasons why missions are cancelled is classified information.

2001
★ Delta operators take part in the invasion of Afghanistan

1991
★ Delta Force carries out missions in the Persian Gulf War

2003
★ Delta Force takes part in the invasion of Iraq

1993
★ Delta Force takes part in military operations in Somalia

2001

2003

DELTA FORCE AROUND THE WORLD

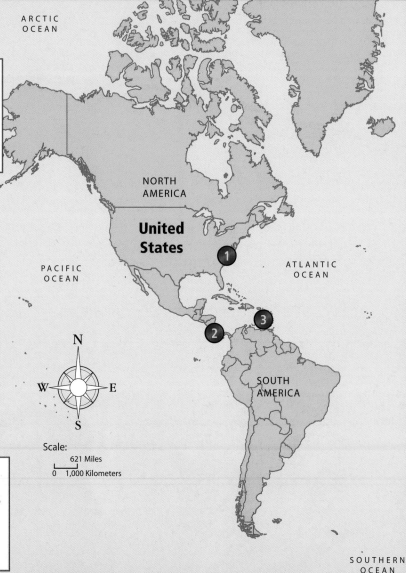

1 North Carolina
Delta Force has headquarters at Fort Bragg, a large U.S. Army base that is home to many other Army units.

2 Panama
In 1989, Delta Force took part in the U.S. invasion of Panama. During the invasion, 23 Delta Force personnel stormed a prison to rescue an American **civilian**.

3 Grenada
In 1983, Delta Force operators were among the first wave of troops in the U.S.-led invasion of Grenada.

Delta Force personnel are stationed at various military bases in the United States as they prepare for missions. When carrying out missions overseas, Delta Force operators use the same bases as other U.S. special forces and other branches of the Armed Forces.

 Iraq

Delta Force operators were involved in the invasion of Iraq in 2003 and many other missions in that country afterwards. They played an important part in the search for, and capture of, Iraqi president Saddam Hussein.

⑤ Middle East

Delta Force units fought in the Persian Gulf War in 1991. Their main mission was to locate and destroy missiles in western Iraq.

ARCTIC
OCEAN

ASIA

EUROPE

⑥ Somalia

In 1993, Delta Force troops were involved in U.S. military operations in Somalia. Delta snipers fought in the Battle of Mogadishu.

④

⑦

⑤

PACIFIC
OCEAN

AFRICA

⑥

INDIAN
OCEAN

⑦ Afghanistan

Delta Force operators took part in the invasion of Afghanistan in 2001. It played a key role in the search for **Osama bin Laden** and other **al-Qaeda** terrorists.

AUSTRALIA

DELTA FORCE UNIFORMS

On combat missions, Delta Force operators wear the U.S. Army combat uniform. Unlike uniforms worn by other members of the Army, Delta Force uniforms have no markings, such as the name of the military unit or the name of the operator.

THE GENEVA CONVENTION

Delta Force operators work on secret missions behind enemy lines. Instead of wearing uniforms like other soldiers, they often dress like local people in order to fit in. They may also wear civilian clothes when they are off duty or at their base. Delta Force operators also have longer hair than other U.S. soldiers and are allowed to grow mustaches and beards. This helps them to blend in with local civilians and not be recognized as soldiers.

The Geneva Convention is an international treaty that protects soldiers who are captured during wartime. Soldiers not wearing uniforms do not have this protection. If captured by the enemy, Delta Force operators working in secret may be treated poorly.

COMBAT UNIFORM

The helmet is made from bullet-resistant material known as Kevlar or Twaron. Goggles protect the eyes. A night-vision device can be attached to the helmet for operations at night or in low-light environments.

The uniform's Universal Camouflage Pattern blends tan, gray, and green and works effectively in desert, woodland, and urban environments. The Improved Outer Tactical Vest, or IOTV body armor, can be worn over the jacket.

The trousers are worn with a 2-inch (5-centimeter) nylon web belt and feature Velcro pouches and two storage pockets at both the thighs and the calves. Operators wear tan-colored combat boots. Operators also wear elbow pads, kneepads, gloves, and protective eyewear.

DELTA FORCE WEAPONS

Delta Force uses some of the same weapons as other units of the U.S. special operations forces. Information about other weapons and equipment is classified.

M4 CARBINE RIFLE

The M4 carbine rifle is one of the main guns used by Delta Force. It is a shorter and lighter version of a similar gun also used by the Army, the M16 assault rifle. The M4 operates on gas and can be fired in **semiautomatic** or in bursts of three rounds. Its barrel is 14.5 inches (37 centimeters) long. The shorter barrel allows the operators to use the rifle better in close-range combat.

M9 BERETTA PISTOL

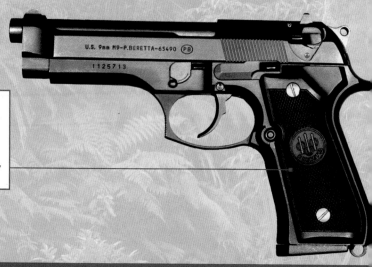

The M9 Beretta is a semiautomatic pistol. It is one of the standard handguns used by the U.S. military. The pistol has a 4.7-inch (12 cm) long barrel and a **magazine** with 15 rounds. The M9 can be fitted with lights, lasers, and other accessories.

M82A1 RIFLE

The M82A1 is a powerful semiautomatic rifle used by Delta Force snipers. It can hit targets at long range and go through body armor and most building materials. The rifle can hit targets behind walls, destroy communication equipment or power generators, and rip into armored vehicles.

HK416 ASSAULT RIFLE

Delta Force now uses the HK416 assault rifle more often than the M4 rifle. The HK416 has a range of 400 yards (365 m) and can fire between 700 and 900 rounds per minute. This rifle is available in four different barrel lengths and can be fitted with scopes, lighting devices, grenade launchers, and other accessories.

JOINING DELTA FORCE

Anyone wishing to join Delta Force must be a male U.S. citizen or permanent resident. To qualify, people must first join the Army and be at least 21 years old. A high school education and the ability to pass the Delta Force physical and mental tests are also required. A college degree is needed to qualify for **officer** training programs. Women are not allowed to join Delta Force.

Applying to the Army

Step One: Apply online

Step Two: Talk to a recruiter about Delta Force

Step Three: Take the Armed Services Vocational Aptitude Battery (ASVAB)

Step Four: Visit the Military Entrance Processing Station (MEPS)

OATH OF ENLISTMENT

❝ I do solemnly swear that I will support and defend the Constitution of the United States against all enemies, foreign and domestic; that I will bear true faith and allegiance to the same; and that I will obey the orders of the President of the United States and the orders of the officers appointed over me, according to regulations and the Uniform Code of Military Justice. So help me God. ❞

Boot Camp Training for Army **recruits** is often called Boot Camp. Many members of Delta Force are recruited from the Green Berets and Army Rangers, or from other units of the Army. Recruits go through a long period of Army training, but still need to do training specifically for Delta Force.

All new Delta Force recruits must go through a selection process that takes three or four weeks. They must pass tough physical tests required for parachuting, underwater swimming, and carrying heavy packs. There are also tests to measure mental toughness. Those who complete these tests go into the Operators Training Course (OTC). The OTC takes six months, after which the recruits join one of the Delta Force squadrons.

JOBS IN DELTA FORCE

Being a Delta Force operator is not just about serving in combat. There are many types of careers in Delta Force and the Army in general. There are jobs in engineering, communications, electronics, medicine, working with computers and technology, and **military intelligence**. The training and experience gained in Delta Force can also lead to successful careers in civilian life after military service is completed.

Communications and Technology

Jobs in this field include working with computers, collecting and studying information, and providing assistance with technology. Delta Force communications experts work with all kinds of communications systems, from radio networks to satellites.

Linguists and Interpreters

Delta Force operators spend much of their military career overseas on missions in foreign countries. There are careers for those with detailed knowledge of different cultures and for linguists who can expertly read, write, and speak foreign languages. Other jobs involve translating and interpreting languages to help military personnel operate more effectively.

Health Care and Medicine

Careers in health care and medicine include working as doctors or nurses. Doctors may be stationed at bases secretly to care for Delta Force personnel. Other jobs involve managing health care facilities, laboratory research, or operating medical tools such as X-ray and ultrasound equipment.

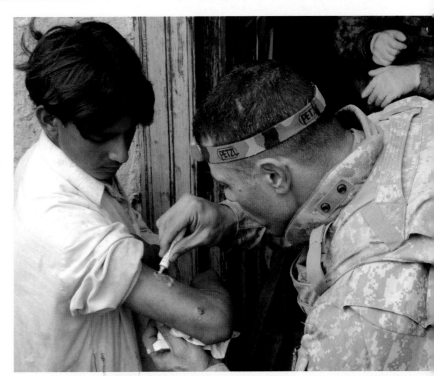

COMMUNITY LIFE

Delta Force operators often work in secret operations overseas, but on military bases, life in Delta Force is much like civilian life. Delta Force operators often work regular hours, and fill their free time with hobbies, sports, and other activities.

Many bases where Delta Force operators are stationed have all the facilities of most towns and cities. This may include hospitals, schools, day care centers, libraries, sports facilities, and shopping malls. Delta Force provides a wide variety of programs to improve the quality of life for personnel living on military bases. These include counseling services, programs to improve on-base education, and programs that help families deal with the stress of having a loved one working in a combat area overseas.

★ Delta Force operators may be away from home for extended periods of time.

WRITE YOUR STORY

If you apply to join the Army and Delta Force, you will probably need to write an essay about yourself. This is also true when you apply to a college or for a job. Practice telling your story by completing this writing activity.

1 Brainstorming

Start by making notes about your interests. What are your hobbies? Do you like to read? Are you more interested in computers or power tools? Then, organize your ideas into an outline, with a clear beginning, middle, and end.

2 Writing the First Draft

A first draft does not have to be perfect. Try to get the story written. Then, read it to see if it makes sense. It will probably need revision. Even the most famous writers edit their work many times before it is completed.

3 Editing

Go through your story and remove anything that is repeated or not needed. Also, add any missing information that should be included. Be sure the text makes sense and is easy to read.

4 Proofreading

The proofreading is where you check spelling, grammar, and punctuation. You will often find mistakes that you missed during the editing stage. Always look for ways to make your writing the best it can be.

5 Submitting Your Story

When your text is finished, it is time to submit your story, along with any other application materials. A good essay will increase your chances of being accepted, whether it be for a school, a job, or Delta Force.

TEST YOUR KNOWLEDGE

1 In what year was Delta Force founded?

2 Where is the headquarters of Delta Force?

3 What assault rifle do Delta Force operators use?

4 When did Delta Force take part in the U.S. invasion of Panama?

5 What does IOTV stand for?

6 What do members of Delta Force call themselves?

7 What is the Geneva Convention?

8 How many people are believed to be in Delta Force?

9 At what age can a person join Delta Force?

10 What is the OTC?

Answers: 1. 1977 2. Fort Bragg, North Carolina 3. The HK416 Assault Rifle 4. 1989 5. Improved Outer Tactical Vest 6. The Unit 7. An international treaty protecting soldiers who are captured during wartime 8. Between 800 and 1,000 9. 21 years old 10. Operators Training Course

KEY WORDS

al-Qaeda: an international terrorist organization founded in Afghanistan in the late 1980s

civilian: a person who is not a member of the armed forces

classified information: military or government information that is kept secret from the public

DEVGRU: The U.S. Naval Special Warfare Development Group, or DEVGRU, is an elite unit of Navy SEALs that carries out missions under the command of Joint Special Operations Command (JSOC)

hostages: people who are held prisoner by an enemy until certain conditions or promises are met

magazine: the part of a firearm in which ammunition is stored and fed into the weapon

military intelligence: information about the armed forces of another country

officer: a soldier who is in a position of authority

Osama bin Laden: the world's most wanted terrorist until he was killed in May 2011

reconnaissance: exploration of an area to gather useful information

recruits: new members of the Armed Forces

semiautomatic: a firing mode in which a gun can fire a single round, or bullet, and load a new round each time the trigger is pulled

snipers: highly trained marksmen who shoot at the enemy from concealed positions or long distances without being detected

terrorism: the use of violence or threats to harm or create fear within a country

INDEX

Log on to www.av2books.com

AV² by Weigl brings you media enhanced books that support active learning. Go to www.av2books.com, and enter the special code found on page 2 of this book. You will gain access to enriched and enhanced content that supplements and complements this book. Content includes video, audio, weblinks, quizzes, a slide show, and activities.

AV² Online Navigation

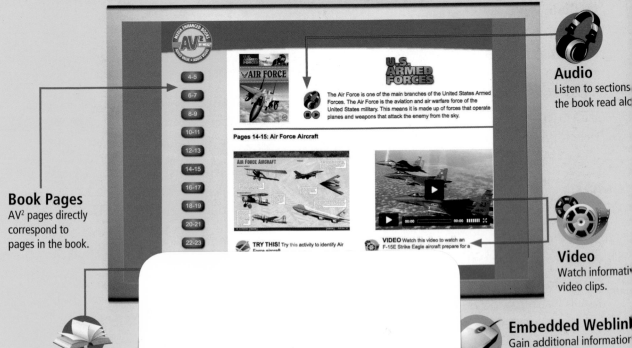

4-5
6-7
8-9
10-11
12-13
14-15
16-17
18-19
20-21
22-23

Book Pages
AV² pages directly correspond to pages in the book.

Audio
Listen to sections the book read al

Video
Watch informati
video clips.

Key Words
Study vocabulary, a
complete a matchi
word activity.

Embedded Weblin
Gain additional informatior
for research.

Try This!
Complete activities and
hands-on experiments.

Q
Te

al. We encourage you
future.

r at

ovided as part of AV² by Weigl may have
h changes. All media enhanced books
ntact AV² by Weigl at 1-866-649-3445

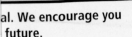